Scottish Salmon

Scottish Salmon

Mary Macdonald

illustrated by

Jacqueline Pestel

HAMLYN

ACKNOWLEDGEMENTS

Art Director Jacqui Small
Designer Louise Leffler
Executive Editor Susan Haynes
Editor Elsa Petersen-Schepelern
Production Controller Melanie Frantz
Illustrator Jacqueline Pestel

First published in 1995 by Hamlyn
an imprint of Reed Consumer Books Limited
Michelin House, 81 Fulham Road, London SW3 6RB
and Auckland, Melbourne, Singapore and Toronto.
Text copyright © 1995 Reed International Books Limited
ISBN 0 600 58480 1
A CIP catalogue record for this book is available at the British Library.
Printed in Hong Kong

NOTES
Both metric and imperial measurements have been given in all recipes.
Use one set of measurements only and not a mixture of both.
Standard level spoon measurements are used in all recipes.
1 tablespoon = one 15 ml spoon   1 teaspoon = one 5 ml spoon
Eggs should be size 3 and milk full fat unless otherwise stated.
Ovens should be preheated to the specified temperature – if using a fan
assisted oven, follow the manufacturer's instructions for adjusting
the time and the temperature.

Contents

Introduction

Salmon is the King of Fish, and Scottish Salmon
is undoubtedly the Emperor.

Cook this marvellous fish for dinner parties,
family meals, summer lunches, or even when
you have guests for breakfast!

Serve salmon in the traditional ways – fresh with
Hollandaise sauce, or smoked with brown bread,
finely sliced onion, freshly ground black pepper
and capers (but never with lemon, which
destroys the delicious smoky taste).

But these are just the beginning – and this book
will take those traditional presentations further.
Try salmon with pasta, in soups, with omelettes,
scrambled eggs and croissants. Try poaching,
frying and baking salmon, or cook it in pies,
mousses, pâtés and terrines.

Wild or farmed, fresh or smoked, salmon is now
within most people's reach, but its extraordinary
quality and flavour ensure that it still retains that
'special occasion' reputation.

Salmon Bouillabaisse

True bouillabaisse can, of course, only be made on the shores of the Mediterranean, but if they had salmon in the Mediterranean, their bouillabaisse would be even better.

500 g/1 lb Scottish salmon and 500 g/1 lb white fish
50 ml/2 fl oz olive oil
2 large onions, finely chopped
1 celery stick, finely sliced
3 garlic cloves, crushed
4 large, ripe tomatoes, skinned, deseeded and chopped
1 bouquet garni, including bay leaves and parsley stalks
rind of 1 small orange
1.8 litres/3 pints fish stock
saffron strands, steeped for 30 minutes in boiling water
about 20 mussels, scrubbed, with beards removed
600 ml/1 pint cooked prawns, peeled
salt and freshly ground black pepper

1 Scale, clean, skin and fillet the fish. Heat the olive oil in a large casserole and fry the onion and celery, then the garlic, until softened but not coloured. Add the tomatoes, bouquet garni, orange rind, stock and saffron mixture. Boil for 5 minutes, add mussels and cook until they open. Discard any mussels which do not open.
2 Add the fish and simmer until it becomes opaque. Add the prawns and heat through. Discard the bouquet garni, season and serve.

Serves 8–10

Scottish Salmon and Avocado Salad

500 G/1 LB COOKED SCOTTISH SALMON,
CHILLED AND CUT INTO STRIPS
1 PACKET MIXED GREEN SALAD LEAVES
2 RIPE AVOCADOS, HALVED, STONED AND PEELED
JUICE OF 1 LEMON

FOR THE VINAIGRETTE:
150 ML/¼ PINT EXTRA-VIRGIN OLIVE OIL
1 TABLESPOON BALSAMIC VINEGAR
1 TABLESPOON LIME JUICE
50 ML/2 FL OZ WINE VINEGAR
1 GARLIC CLOVE, CRUSHED
1 TEASPOON DIJON MUSTARD
A PINCH OF SUGAR
SALT AND FRESHLY GROUND BLACK PEPPER
1 TEASPOON CHOPPED FRESH PARSLEY OR CHIVES
SPRIGS OF BASIL, TO GARNISH

1 Place all the ingredients for the vinaigrette in a screw top jar and
shake vigorously to emulsify. Toss the mixed salad leaves with
4 tablespoons of vinaigrette, and place a little salad on each plate.
2 Slice the avocados into a fan shape. Place one half decoratively on
each plate. Sprinkle with lemon juice to prevent discoloration.
3 Place the fish beside the avocado, and drizzle over a little extra
vinaigrette, season to taste and garnish with sprigs of basil.

Serves 4

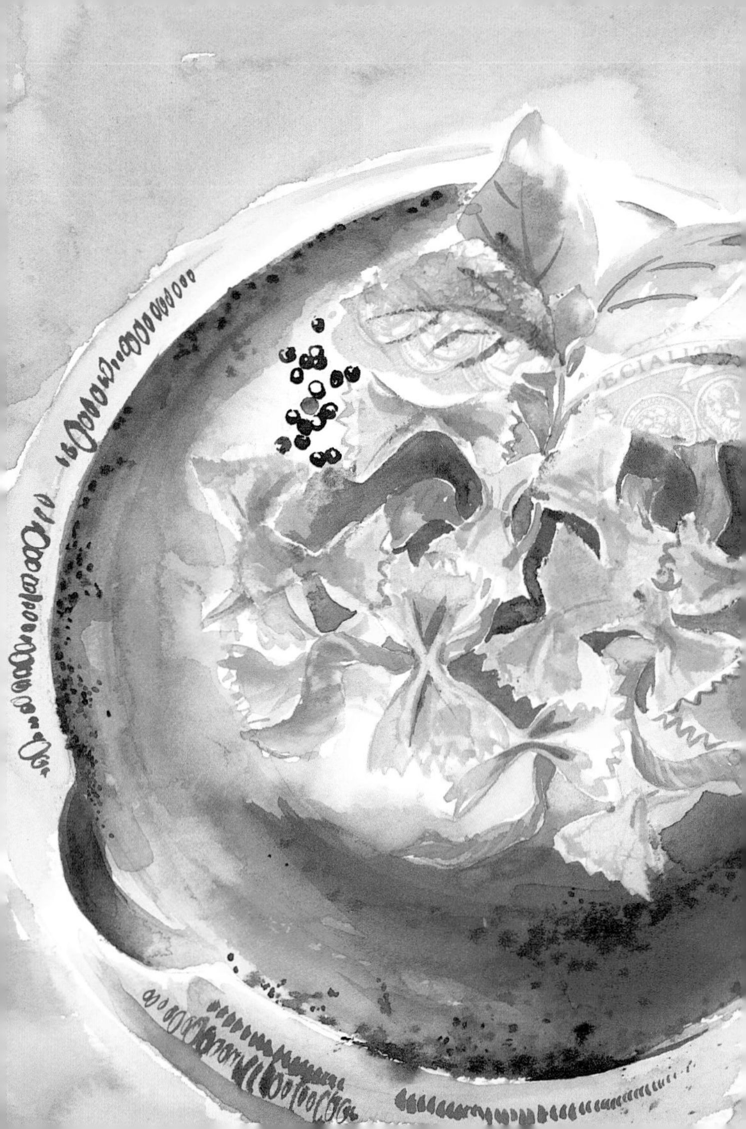

Pasta with Smoked Salmon and Basil

6 TABLESPOONS FULL-FAT SOFT CHEESE, AT ROOM TEMPERATURE

6 TABLESPOONS NATURAL YOGURT

350 G/12 OZ SMOKED SALMON, CUT INTO SHORT STRIPS

2 TABLESPOONS FINELY CHOPPED FRESH BASIL

350 G/12 OZ PASTA SHELLS OR BOWS

2 TABLESPOONS WALNUT OIL

FRESHLY GRATED NUTMEG

SALT AND FRESHLY GROUND BLACK PEPPER

BASIL SPRIGS, TO GARNISH

1 Mash the cheese with the yogurt until smooth and creamy.
Add the smoked salmon strips and chopped basil, mix well and leave to
stand while cooking the pasta.

2 Cook the pasta in a large pan of salted water for 6-8 minutes
if dried and 3-4 minutes if fresh – until *al dente*.
Drain thoroughly and return to the rinsed-out pan.

3 Stir the walnut oil into the pasta over a medium heat, then
stir in the cheese and yogurt mixture until very hot.

4 Season with freshly ground black pepper and nutmeg
and garnish with basil.

Serves 6

Fresh Salmon Pâté

750 G/1½ LB FRESH SCOTTISH SALMON, POACHED AS
ON PAGE 33, AND COOLED

175 G/6 OZ UNSALTED BUTTER, SOFTENED

FOR THE SAUCE:

75 G/3 OZ BUTTER

75 G/3 OZ PLAIN FLOUR

600 ML/1 PINT MILK

2 TEASPOONS LEMON JUICE

SALT AND FRESHLY GROUND BLACK PEPPER

TO GARNISH:

½ CUCUMBER, CUT INTO THIN RINGS

1 HARD-BOILED EGG, YOLK CRUMBLED, WHITE CHOPPED

1 TABLESPOON CHOPPED FRESH PARSLEY

1 To make the sauce, melt the butter in a saucepan, remove from the
heat and stir in the flour. Cook the roux for 2-3 minutes, then
gradually add the milk, beating well between each addition until really
smooth. Simmer gently for 3-4 minutes, add the lemon juice,
salt and pepper and allow to cool.

2 Cream the butter. Skin and flake the cooked salmon and process
until smooth, then mix in the sauce and the creamed butter.
Spoon into a pâté dish, cover with clingfilm and chill.

3 To serve, unmould the salmon, arrange the cucumber around the
pâté, sprinkle with the chopped egg white, egg yolk and parsley.

Serves 12

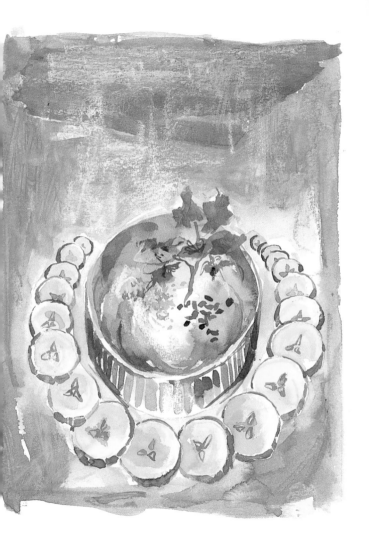

Salmon and Avocado Mousse

FOR THE SALMON MOUSSE:
125 G/4 OZ FRESH COOKED SALMON, PURÉED
150 ML/¼ PINT COLD BÉCHAMEL OR WHITE SAUCE
4 TABLESPOONS MAYONNAISE
1½ TEASPOONS POWDERED GELATINE, DISSOLVED
3 TABLESPOONS DOUBLE CREAM

FOR THE AVOCADO MOUSSE:
1 AVOCADO, HALVED, STONED, PEELED AND MASHED OR PURÉED
2 TEASPOONS WORCESTERSHIRE SAUCE
2 TEASPOONS FINELY GRATED ONION
½ TEASPOON SALT
150 ML/¼ PINT HOT CHICKEN STOCK
1½ TEASPOONS POWDERED GELATINE, DISSOLVED
3 TABLESPOONS MAYONNAISE
3 TABLESPOONS DOUBLE CREAM

1 For the salmon mousse, mix the first 4 ingredients, then add the gelatine and stir in the cream.

2 For the avocado mousse, mix the avocado with the Worcestershire sauce, onion and salt, blend in the stock, then stir in the gelatine. Stir over ice until cold, then add the mayonnaise and cream.

3 Pour half the salmon into an oiled 18 cm/7 inch ring mould. Set in the freezer. After 10 minutes, add half the avocado mixture and set. Add the remainder of the salmon, set, then the final layer of avocado. Set, refrigerate, then unmould and serve.

Serves 4

Timbales of Smoked Salmon

125 g/4 oz SMOKED SALMON, THINLY SLICED
125 ml/4 fl oz CRÈME FRAÎCHE, CHILLED
2 TABLESPOONS RED CAVIAR OR SALMON ROE
PINCH OF CAYENNE OR DASH OF TABASCO SAUCE, TO TASTE
FOR THE FRESH TOMATO PURÉE:
4 RIPE TOMATOES, SKINNED, DESEEDED AND CHOPPED
SALT AND FRESHLY GROUND BLACK PEPPER
TO GARNISH:
SNIPPED FRESH CHIVES OR FRESH DILL
WHOLE FRESH CHIVES OR SPRIGS OF FRESH DILL

1 Rinse 4 small soufflé dishes and line with dampened greaseproof paper. Line with slices of smoked salmon and trim them level with the rims. Chop the trimmings finely. Beat the crème fraîche until soft peaks form, and fold in the chopped salmon, caviar and cayenne pepper or Tabasco sauce.

2 Fill the moulds, cover and chill overnight.

3 Purée the tomato flesh then rub through a fine sieve. Season with salt and pepper and chill.

4 Unmould the timbales on to individual serving plates and spoon a circle of tomato purée around each one. Sprinkle with snipped chives or dill and garnish with whole chives or sprigs of dill.

Serves 4

Potted Salmon

A fine breakfast dish with toast – beautiful when served in pretty ceramic pots.

1 TEASPOON VINEGAR
500 G/1 LB FRESH SCOTTISH SALMON
1 TEASPOON LEMON JUICE
125 G/4 OZ BUTTER
A PINCH OF GROUND MACE
3 TABLESPOONS MELTED BUTTER

1 Add the vinegar to the water of a steamer and steam the salmon for about 5 minutes, or until the fish leaves the bones.

2 Remove the skin and bones and flake the fish, then blend the fish with the lemon juice, butter and mace.

3 Press into 4 little pots. If the fish is not to be eaten at once, pour the melted butter over the tops and let it set firmly. Serve with toast or brown bread and butter.

Serves 4

Layered Salmon Terrine

250 G/8 OZ SALMON, BONES AND SKIN REMOVED

300 ML/½ PINT DOUBLE CREAM

3 EGGS

1 TABLESPOON CHOPPED DILL

SALT AND FRESHLY GROUND BLACK PEPPER

25 G/1 OZ BUTTER

50 G/2 OZ PINE NUTS

250 G/8 OZ UNCOOKED PRAWNS, PEELED AND DEVEINED

250 G/8 OZ SPINACH LEAVES, WASHED, BLANCHED AND DRIED

SPRIGS OF DILL, TO GARNISH

1 Purée the fish, cream, eggs, dill, salt and pepper until smooth and creamy. Remove and set aside.

2 In a small pan, melt the butter and sauté the pine nuts for a few seconds until golden. Process the prawns for a few seconds, remove, mix in the pine nuts, and season to taste.

3 Grease a 1 kg/2 lb terrine and line with spinach leaves, leaving enough to wrap over the top. Pour in half the salmon mixture, add a layer of spinach, a layer of prawn mixture, and another layer of spinach. Pour in the remaining salmon mixture and fold the spinach over the top. Cover with foil, place in a 'bain-marie' and cook in a preheated oven at 160°C (325°F) Gas Mark 3 for 40-50 minutes, until the terrine is firm to the touch.

4 Remove and cool before unmoulding. Chill for 2 hours before serving, cut into slices and garnish with sprigs of dill.

Serves 8

Scottish Gravad Lax

LARGE BUNCH OF FRESH DILL, FINELY CHOPPED

1 x 1 KG/2¼ LB MIDDLE-CUT OF FRESH SALMON,
SKINNED, BONED, CUT INTO 2 FILLETS, AND DRIED THOROUGHLY

65 G/2½ OZ CASTER SUGAR

10 BLACK PEPPERCORNS, CRUSHED AND 65 G/2½ OZ COARSE SEA SALT

FOR THE SAUCE:

2 TABLESPOONS GERMAN MUSTARD

1 EGG YOLK

1 TABLESPOON CASTER SUGAR

2 TABLESPOONS WHITE WINE VINEGAR

7 TABLESPOONS OLIVE OIL

1 TABLESPOON CHOPPED FRESH DILL

SALT AND FRESHLY GROUND BLACK PEPPER

LEMON SLICES AND SPRIGS OF FRESH DILL, TO GARNISH

1 Sprinkle a little dill on the base of a large shallow dish.

2 Rub the salmon all over with the sugar. Put one of the fillets into the dish, sprinkle with more dill, all the peppercorns and half the salt. Cover with the second fillet, remaining salt and more dill.

3 Cover with clingfilm, weight heavily and chill for 2-5 days.

4 To make the sauce, beat the mustard with the egg yolk, sugar and vinegar. Slowly beat in the oil, drop by drop, until thickened and well blended. Add dill, salt and pepper.

5 Slice the salmon paper-thin and serve with a little mustard sauce. Garnish with lemon slices and sprigs of dill.

Serves 6-8

Scottish Sashimi

*The Japanese have a passion for fresh, good-quality fish.
Scottish Salmon is the finest of all British fish and makes a
sumptuous addition to this Caledonian version of sashimi.*

750 G/1½ LB MIXED FRESH FISH,
SUCH AS SALMON, SOLE, SEA BASS AND TUNA
CLEANED, WASHED, FILLETED AND DRIED
1 TEASPOON WASABI POWDER OR 2 TEASPOONS WASABI PASTE
SOY SAUCE
5 CM/2 INCH PIECE DAIKON (JAPANESE WHITE RADISH),
PEELED AND SHREDDED
PLAIN BOILED JAPANESE RICE, TO SERVE

1 Slice the fish into pieces with a very sharp knife – salmon and sole
should be sliced very thinly, sea bass about 1 cm/½ inch thick,
and tuna into bite-sized pieces.

2 Put the wasabi powder into an egg cup, add 1 teaspoon cold water
and stir. Keep covered so the flavour does not escape.
Pour the soy sauce into individual small dishes.

3 To serve, arrange the different fishes decoratively on a serving
platter, and garnish with the shredded daikon. Mould the wasabi into
a small mound and place on the platter. Guests take a little wasabi in
their chopsticks, mix it into their soy sauce and dip slices of sashimi
into the sauce before eating. Boiled rice is eaten between
mouthfuls to cool the palate.

Serves 4

Scrambled Eggs with Scottish Smoked Salmon

A marvellous way to serve scrambled eggs for a celebration breakfast or 'brunch' – with hot buttered toast, freshly-squeezed orange juice, and good, strong coffee.

8-10 EGGS

8-10 TABLESPOONS MILK OR CREAM (1 TABLESPOON PER EGG)

SALT AND FRESHLY GROUND BLACK PEPPER

125 G/4 OZ UNSALTED BUTTER

8 SLICES SMOKED SALMON

TO GARNISH:

2 TABLESPOONS CHOPPED, FRESH, FLAT LEAF PARSLEY,

OR SNIPPED FRESH CHIVES

1 Break the eggs in to a bowl, add the milk or cream, season with salt and pepper, and beat with a fork.

2 Melt the butter in a small saucepan, preferably non-stick, until it foams slightly. Add the eggs, cook over a low heat, stirring with a wooden spoon or spatula. Keep stirring as the eggs cook, scraping them away from the base and sides.

3 When the eggs are set but still creamy, remove from the heat and serve at once on warmed dinner plates. Place two slices of smoked salmon beside the eggs, and garnish with chopped parsley or snipped chives.

Serves 4

French Omelette with Scottish Salmon, Cream and Cheese

*Another example of the 'Auld Alliance'
between Scotland and France!*

FOR THE FILLING:

50 G/2 OZ SMOKED SALMON, CUT INTO STRIPS,
OR COOKED SALMON, FLAKED

1 TABLESPOON CREAM

1 SPRING ONION, FINELY SLICED

1 TABLESPOON GRATED CHEESE

FOR THE OMELETTE

3 EGGS, AT ROOM TEMPERATURE

1 TABLESPOON WATER

15 G/½ OZ UNSALTED BUTTER

SALT AND FRESHLY GROUND BLACK PEPPER

SPRIGS OF PARSLEY OR SNIPPED CHIVES, TO GARNISH

1 In a small pan, heat the salmon, cream, spring onion and cheese.

2 Gently beat the eggs and water together and season to taste.

3 Melt the butter in a pan, pour in the eggs and, with a fork, pull the mixture from the edge towards the centre, allowing the uncooked mixture to run to the outside. When the eggs have set underneath, but the top still quite creamy, spoon the filling along the middle of the omelette, then fold over one-third. Fold over again, and slide on to a heated plate. Garnish with sprigs of parsley or snipped chives.

Serves 1

Croissants with Avocado and Smoked Salmon

This recipe comes from Queensland, in tropical Australia, where avocados 'grow on trees'. Locals know that one of the nicest ways to have this delicious fruit is on toast, with crispy bacon or smoked salmon. This is a more sumptuous version of that original – ideal for Sunday breakfast with strong coffee and good newspapers.

8 BUTTER CROISSANTS
8 SLICES SMOKED SALMON (OR MORE IF LIKED)
4 LARGE RIPE AVOCADOS, HALVED (HAAS IS THE BEST VARIETY)
8 TEASPOONS SALMON ROE OR CAVIAR (OPTIONAL)
FRESHLY GROUND BLACK PEPPER

1 Warm the croissants in the oven at 220°C (425°F) Gas Mark 7, remove and split in half lengthways, leaving a 'hinge', like a book. Cut the smoked salmon diagonally into strips.

2 Scrape out the avocado flesh, including the bright green parts, and heap generously over one half of each croissant.

3 Place in the oven for a few minutes until the avocado is warm.

4 Remove and place on a serving plate. Arrange slices of smoked salmon attractively on top of the avocado. Sprinkle with pepper.

5 Press the top half of each croissant at an angle on top of the avocado and salmon. Garnish with salmon roe or caviar, if liked.

Serves 8

Poached Salmon Cutlets
with Hot Basil Sauce

4 CELERY STICKS, CHOPPED

1 CARROT, PEELED AND CHOPPED

1 SMALL ONION, PEELED AND CHOPPED

1 LARGE BUNCH FRESH BASIL, LEAVES STRIPPED FROM STALKS

6 SALMON CUTLETS OR STEAKS, ABOUT
125 G/4 OZ EACH AND 2.5 CM/1 INCH THICK

75 ML/3 FL OZ WHITE WINE

125 ML/4 FL OZ WATER

SALT AND FRESHLY GROUND BLACK PEPPER

1 TEASPOON LEMON JUICE

15 G/½ OZ UNSALTED BUTTER

SALT AND FRESHLY GROUND BLACK PEPPER

1 Spread all the vegetables over the bottom of a large flameproof dish,
bed the salmon cutlets into the vegetables and cover them
with half the basil. Reserve the remaining basil.

2 Pour over the wine and water, season, bring to the boil, cover and
simmer for 10 minutes. Place the salmon on a warmed serving dish.

3 Bring the liquid back to the boil and simmer for 5 minutes. Strain
into a liquidizer. Add the cooked and uncooked basil, and purée. Place
in a pan, bring to the boil and reduce by half, until thickened.

4 Remove from the heat, stir in the lemon juice and butter, pour over
the salmon cutlets and serve.

Serves 6

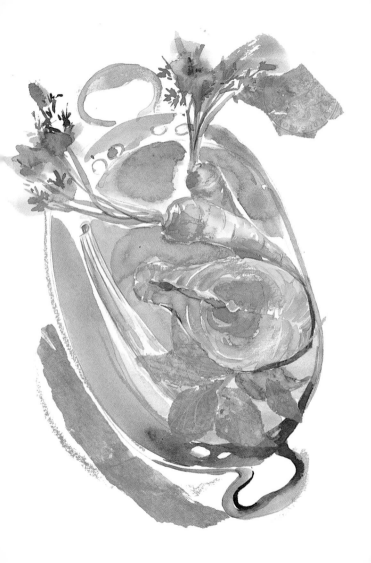

Poached Salmon

A recipe for a large party, easily adapted for smaller numbers.

1 SALMON, ABOUT 5.5 KG / 12 LB

FOR THE COURT BOUILLON:

1.8 LITRES / 3 PINTS COLD WATER

1 MEDIUM ONION, FINELY SLICED

1 CARROT, FINELY SLICED

3 SPRIGS PARSLEY

3 SPRIGS THYME

3 SPRIGS TARRAGON

1 BAY LEAF

1 TEASPOON SALT

5 PEPPERCORNS

1 TABLESPOON OLIVE OIL

1 SMALL CUCUMBER, PEELED AND THINLY SLICED, TO GARNISH

1 Pour the water for the court bouillon into a fish kettle with all the other ingredients except the olive oil. Boil for 30 minutes.

2 Remove from the heat and add the olive oil. Carefully lower the salmon into the liquid, which should just cover it.

3 Bring back to the boil, then simmer very gently for 30 minutes, or until the salmon flesh leaves the bone easily. Lift out on to a flat serving dish, garnish with thin slices of cucumber and serve hot with Hollandaise sauce, or cold with Mayonnaise and a cucumber salad. To serve cold, cool in the liquid, lift out and chill.

Serves 24 or more

Whole Salmon in Aspic

1 SCOTTISH SALMON, 2 KG/4 LB,
CLEANED AND SCALED, WITH THE HEAD AND TAIL LEFT ON,
POACHED IN WATER TO COVER, AS IN THE PREVIOUS RECIPE
1 TABLESPOON MADEIRA OR DRY SHERRY
2 TABLESPOONS POWDERED GELATINE
3-4 SPRIGS OF FRESH TARRAGON
1 SMALL CUCUMBER, THINLY SLICED

1 Poach, cool and chill the fish. Skin the salmon, leaving the head
and tail on, and transfer to a serving platter.

2 Strain the stock into a clean saucepan, boil and skim while
reducing to 600 ml/1 pint. Cool for 10-15 minutes then blot any fat
off the surface with paper towels. Stir in the Madeira or sherry.

3 Mix the gelatine with 3 tablespoons water in a bowl and stand over
simmering water until dissolved. Whisk into the stock and leave until
just beginning to set (the consistency of egg whites).

4 Dip tarragon sprigs into the setting aspic and arrange down the
length of the fish. Dip cucumber slices in aspic and arrange some in a
'collar' at the head end, and some at the tail end. Leave until set.

5 Coat the fish with a thin layer of aspic and leave until set.
Repeat the process, using all the aspic.

6 When set, dip a sharp thin-bladed knife into cold water, and cut
through the aspic right around the fish. Scrape the aspic off the
platter, chop finely and sprinkle over the fish.

Wipe the platter clean and serve.

Serves 8

Salmon Steaks with Fennel

Equally delicious with salmon cutlets, as illustrated.

2 HEADS FLORENCE FENNEL

2 SALMON STEAKS, ABOUT 750 G/1½ LB TOTAL, SKINNED, BONED
AND CUT IN HALF HORIZONTALLY TO MAKE 4 PIECES – OR 4 CUTLETS

SALT AND FRESHLY GROUND BLACK PEPPER

150 ML/¼ PINT FISH STOCK

150 ML/¼ PINT DRY WHITE WINE

1 TABLESPOON SOFTENED BUTTER, MIXED WITH

1 TABLESPOON PLAIN FLOUR

2 TABLESPOONS DOUBLE CREAM

1 Trim the fennel, cut into 4 slices downwards, reserving the leaves.
Cook in slightly salted water for about 15 minutes.

2 Drain the fennel well, then place in a shallow ovenproof dish.
Lay the salmon on top. Sprinkle with salt and pepper. Pour the fish
stock and wine over the top of the salmon. Cover with foil and
cook in a preheated oven at 180°C (350°F) Gas Mark 4
for 20 minutes.

3 Remove the foil, and transfer the salmon and fennel to a warmed
serving dish. Keep warm, whilst making the sauce.

4 Put the fish stock and wine into a small saucepan and stir in the
butter and flour mixture, a little at a time. Bring to the boil,
whisking well. Cook for 2-3 minutes, then add the double cream.

5 Pour over the salmon, garnish with fennel leaves, and serve.

Serves 4

Salmon Herb Parcels

*'Parcels' of foil seal in the flavour and goodness. The flavour is
stronger in parsley stalks than in the leaves – use them when the
herbs are to be discarded after cooking.*

4 SALMON CUTLETS OR STEAKS

50 G/2 OZ BUTTER

2 BAY LEAVES, HALVED

4 PARSLEY STALKS, BRUISED

4 ONION SLICES

4 SLIVERS OF LEMON RIND

4 THYME SPRIGS

SALT AND FRESHLY GROUND BLACK PEPPER

SPRIGS OF WATERCRESS, TO GARNISH

1 Place each piece of salmon on a square of foil, large enough to
enclose the whole steak. Place a knob of butter on each one and top
with ½ bay leaf, 1 parsley sprig, 1 onion slice, 1 sliver of lemon rind
and 1 thyme sprig. Season to taste. Wrap the steaks or cutlets in
the foil, then place in an ovenproof dish.

2 Barely cover the bottom of the dish with water and bake in a
preheated oven at 180°C (350°F) Gas Mark 4 for 15-20 minutes or
until the salmon is tender. Test with a fork – the flesh should be
opaque, and flake easily.

3 Remove the 'parcels' from the dish, unwrap, and discard the herbs
and seasonings before serving, garnished with watercress.

Serves 4

Salmon in Red Wine

6 SALMON CUTLETS, ABOUT 2.5 CM/1 INCH THICK
125-150 G/4-5 OZ BUTTER
6 SHALLOTS, FINELY CHOPPED
SMALL BUNCH FRESH PARSLEY, FINELY CHOPPED
1 GARLIC CLOVE, PEELED AND FINELY CHOPPED
6 BLACK PEPPERCORNS, CRUSHED
SEA SALT
300 ML/½ PINT RED WINE
SPRIG OF PARSLEY, TO GARNISH

1 Rinse the salmon quickly in cold water, then pat dry.
2 Melt 50 g/2 oz of the butter in a large flameproof dish into which the salmon will fit snugly. Add the shallots and cook gently for 2 minutes, then put in the cutlets and brown for 1 minute on each side over a high heat.
3 Sprinkle over the remaining ingredients, cover with a butter paper and cook in the preheated oven for 10-15 minutes until the salmon is just done.
4 Pour off the cooking juices into a small saucepan. Meanwhile, keep the salmon warm. Cut the rest of the butter into small pieces and whisk into the pan, one at a time, constantly beating until each piece has melted. Stop when the sauce is smooth and glossy. Pour immediately over the salmon, garnish and serve.

Serves 6

Colonial Salmon Kedgeree

Kedgeree is a version of an Indian dish – Khichri – and was first brought back to Britain by members of the East India Company. It was a famous breakfast or supper dish in Scotland in the 18th and 19th Centuries. Usually made with smoked haddock, this recipe comes from a Scottish cook who lives in Tanzania. It is perfect for using cold poached or baked fish left over from other recipes.

125 G/4 OZ RICE

60 G/2 OZ BUTTER

250 G/8 OZ COOKED FRESH OR SMOKED SALMON
WITH SKIN AND BONE REMOVED, FLAKED

2 HARD-BOILED EGGS, FINELY CHOPPED

2-3 TABLESPOONS CREAM

SALT AND FRESHLY GROUND BLACK PEPPER

1 TABLESPOON CHOPPED FRESH FLAT LEAF PARSLEY, TO GARNISH

1 Boil the rice in the usual way, and drain.
2 Melt half the butter in a saucepan, add the salmon, eggs and cream, and toss through until hot. Mix gently with the rice, and add salt and pepper to taste.
3 To serve, pile the kedgeree on to a hot serving plate, dot with the remaining butter and sprinkle with the chopped parsley
4 Serve very hot, with hot buttered toast.

Serves 4

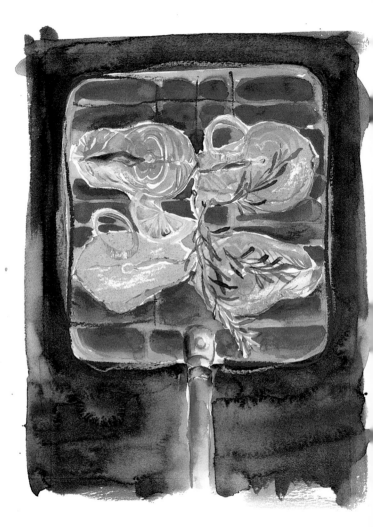

Barbecued Salmon

*Salmon is an excellent fish for cooking on the barbecue.
It holds its shape very well, and its flavour is enhanced by the
slightly toasty, crispy aromas of the smoking herbs. This dish is
based on an Italian recipe, and if you don't have a barbecue, it is
just as delicious – if a little different – cooked under the grill.*

4 SALMON STEAKS OR CUTLETS
150 ML/¼ PINT EXTRA VIRGIN OLIVE OIL
JUICE OF 2 LEMONS
1 SMALL ONION, SLICED
2 GARLIC CLOVES, CRUSHED
1 TABLESPOON CHOPPED FRESH ROSEMARY
2 FRESH BAY LEAVES OR 1 DRIED, TORN INTO PIECES
FRESHLY GROUND BLACK PEPPER

1 Place the salmon in a glass or china dish, and sprinkle with the olive
oil, lemon juice, sliced onion, garlic, rosemary, bay leaves and freshly
ground black pepper. Marinate for at least 30 minutes or overnight in
the refrigerator, turning at least once.

2 Grill under a very hot grill or on a barbecue for about 2 minutes
each side until the fish is lightly cooked inside and slightly crisped
outside. Paint the fish liberally with the marinade as you turn it.

3 Serve with a crisp green salad and potatoes pan-fried with garlic and
fresh rosemary sprigs.

Serves 4

Pan-fried Salmon
with Tomato Coulis

4 FRESH SALMON STEAKS OR CUTLETS, SEASONED WITH SALT,
FRESHLY GROUND BLACK PEPPER AND GRATED NUTMEG

1 GARLIC CLOVE, CRUSHED

2 TABLESPOONS OLIVE OIL

1 SMALL GLASS CLARET (OPTIONAL)

FOR THE TOMATO COULIS:

1.5 KG/3 LB RIPE TOMATOES, SLICED

1 SMALL ONION, FINELY CHOPPED

1 TEASPOON SUGAR

BOUQUET GARNI

JUICE OF 1 LEMON

SALT AND FRESHLY GROUND BLACK PEPPER

1 Place all the ingredients for the tomato coulis, except the lemon juice, into a pan and bring to the boil. Reduce the heat, cover and simmer until very soft. Remove the bouquet garni.

2 Purée, then press through a sieve. Return to the boil and reduce to a sauce-like consistency. Add lemon juice and season to taste.

3 Sauté the garlic in the oil for a few minutes. Remove. Add the salmon and sauté at a high heat for a few seconds on either side. Reduce the heat and cook until the fish is cooked through. Remove and keep warm. Deglaze the pan with the claret; add to the coulis.

4 Place a slice of salmon on to each individual plate and spoon over the tomato coulis. Serve with a salad of mixed green leaves.

Serves 4

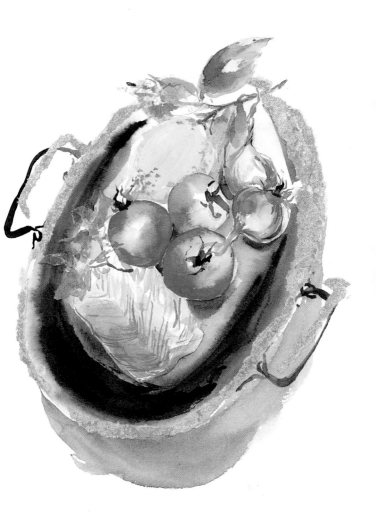

Salmon Fishcakes

Fishcakes are an excellent way of using up leftover cooked or canned fish. Making them with salmon is just a little more luxurious.

250 G/8 OZ FLAKED COOKED SALMON
250 G/8 OZ MASHED POTATOES
1 EGG, BEATEN
1 TABLESPOON CHOPPED FRESH HERBS
SALT AND FRESHLY GROUND BLACK PEPPER, TO TASTE
2 TABLESPOONS OLIVE OIL OR OLIVE OIL AND BUTTER

TO COAT:
4 TABLESPOONS FLOUR
1 EGG, BEATEN
6 TABLESPOONS FINE BREADCRUMBS
SALT AND FRESHLY GROUND BLACK PEPPER

1 Mix the salmon, mashed potatoes, beaten egg, chopped herbs and seasoning, and form into 8 round, flat cakes.

2 Coat them in seasoned flour, then beaten egg and fine breadcrumbs. Add more flour or breadcrumbs if necessary.

3 Heat the oil – or the mixture of oil and butter – in a frying pan and cook the fishcakes until crisp and brown on both sides.

4 Drain on absorbent kitchen paper.

5 Serve hot with slices of lemon, and lots of creamy, buttery mashed potatoes.

Serves 4

Salmon Koulibiac

A fish pie with Russian ancestry.

625 G/1¼ LB SALMON
6 TABLESPOONS MILK
125 G/4 OZ MUSHROOMS, SLICED
1 LARGE ONION, CHOPPED
75 G/3 OZ BROWN RICE, COOKED
1 TABLESPOON CHOPPED PARSLEY
1 x 350 G/13 OZ PACKET FROZEN PUFF PASTRY, THAWED
BEATEN EGG TO GLAZE
SALT AND PEPPER

1 Put the salmon in a saucepan with the milk, salt and pepper. Bring to the boil, reduce the heat, cover and simmer for 5 minutes. Leave to cool in the pan. Drain, reserving the liquid. Flake the fish, and discard the skin and bones. Carefully mix the salmon with the mushrooms, onion, rice and parsley to make the filling.

2 Roll out the pastry to 37 x 33 cm/15 x 13 inches and trim the edges. Cut into 2 strips, one 15 cm/6 inches, the other 18 cm/ 7 inches wide. Put the narrower strip on a baking sheet and cover with the filling, to within 1.5 cm/¾ inch of the edges. Dampen the edges and cover with the remaining pastry, sealing the edges. Decorate with leaves cut from the trimmings.

3 Brush with egg and bake in a preheated oven at 200°C (400°F) Gas Mark 6 for 30 minutes, until golden brown.

Serves 6

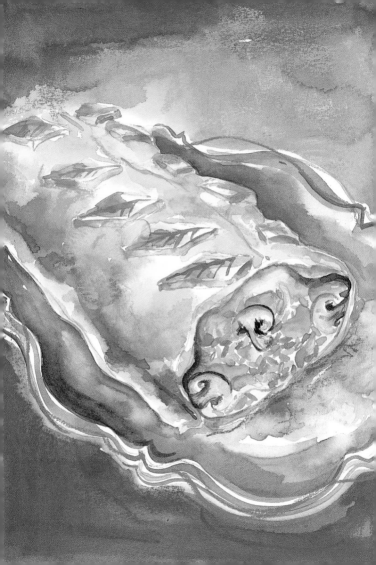

Salmon Pie

With salmon, the homely fish pie becomes a special dish.

1 KG/2 LB POTATOES, CUT INTO CHUNKS
750 G/1½ LB SALMON, SKINNED AND CUT INTO 4 EQUAL PIECES.
900 ML/ 1½ PINTS MILK
75 G/3 OZ BUTTER
40 G/1½ OZ PLAIN FLOUR
SALT AND FRESHLY GROUND BLACK PEPPER

1 Boil and mash the potatoes, and beat with 40 g/1½ oz butter and
150 ml/¼ pint milk until soft and creamy. Set aside to cool.

2 Grease a wide, shallow, ovenproof dish and place the fish in two
layers. Season with salt and pepper and pour over the rest of the milk.
Closely cover with foil and bake in a preheated oven at
180°C (350°F) Gas Mark 4 for 25 minutes.

3 Make a roux with the flour and 25 g/1 oz of the butter,
then remove from the heat. Strain the cooking liquid from the fish
andgradually stir it into the butter and flour mixture. Return to the
heat and cook, stirring for 2–3 minutes. Season to taste and
add the double cream.

4 Pour the sauce evenly over the fish and leave to cool completely.
Spoon the potato over the fish and lightly smooth the surface.
Dot with the remaining butter, and bake near the top of a preheated
oven at 200°C (400°F) Gas Mark 6, for about 25 minutes, until the
fish is heated through and the topping is browned.

Serves 6

Index

Weights and Measures

In this book, both metric and Imperial measures are used.
When working from the recipes, follow one set of measures only,
and not a mixture of both, as they are not interchangeable.

Notes for American and Australian Users
In America, the 8 fl oz measuring cup is used. In Australia, metric
measures are used in conjunction with the standard 250 ml measuring
cup. The Imperial pint, used in Britain and Australia, is 20 fl oz,
while the American pint is 16 fl oz.

The British standard tablespoon, which has been used throughout this
book, holds 17.7 ml, the American 14.2 ml, and the Australian 20 ml.
A teaspoon holds approximately 5 ml in all three countries.

British	American	Australian
1 teaspoon	1 teaspoon	1 teaspoon
1 tablespoons	1 tablespoon	1 tablespoon
2 tablespoons	3 tablespoons	2 tablespoons
3½ tablespoons	4 tablespoons	3 tablespoons
4 tablespoons	5 tablespoons	3½ tablespoons

An Imperial/American Guide to Solid and Liquid Measures

Imperial	American	Imperial	American
Solid Measures		*Liquid Measures*	
1 lb butter	2 cups	¼ pint	⅔ cup
1 lb flour	4 cups	½ pint	1¼ cups
1 lb granulated		¾ pint	2 cups
sugar or caster		1 pint	2½ cups
sugar	2 cups	1½ pints	3¾ cups
1 lb icing sugar	3 cups	2 pints	5 cups
8 oz rice	1 cup		(2½ pints)